Teaching Little Fingers to Play More Easy Duets

9 Equal-Level Duets arranged by

Carolyn Miller

Cover Design by Nick Gressle

ISBN 978-1-4234-8330-4

WILLIS MUSIC

EXCLUSIVELY DISTRIBUTED BY

7777 W. BLUEMOUND RD. P.O. BOX 13819 MILWAUKEE, WI 53213

Visit Hal Leonard Online at
www.halleonard.com

CONTENTS

The Man on the Flying Trapeze

SECONDO

Words by George Leybourne
Music by Alfred Lee
Arranged by Carolyn Miller

Play both hands one octave lower.

The Man on the Flying Trapeze

PRIMO

Words by George Leybourne
Music by Alfred Lee
Arranged by Carolyn Miller

Play both hands one octave higher.

Moderato, in 1

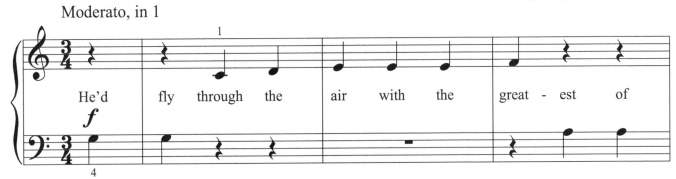

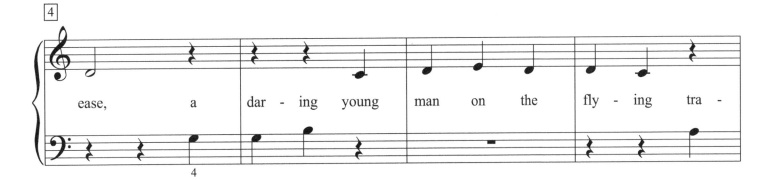

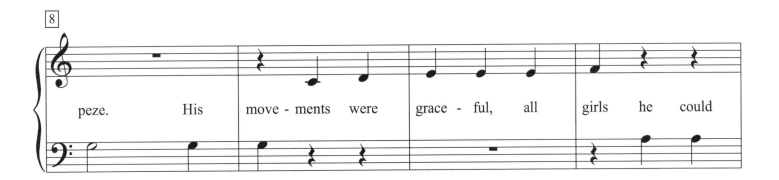

Do Your Ears Hang Low?

SECONDO

Play both hands one octave lower.

Traditional
Arranged by Carolyn Miller

With energy

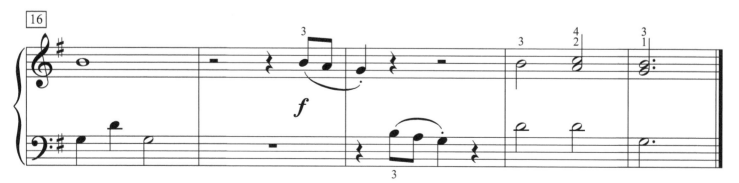

Do Your Ears Hang Low?

PRIMO

Traditional
Arranged by Carolyn Miller

Play both hands one octave higher.

With energy

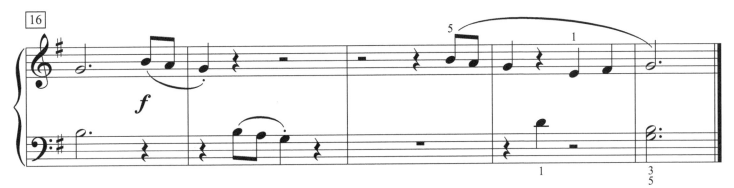

Chopsticks

SECONDO

Play both hands one octave lower.

By Arthur de Lulli*
Arranged by Carolyn Miller

Not too fast

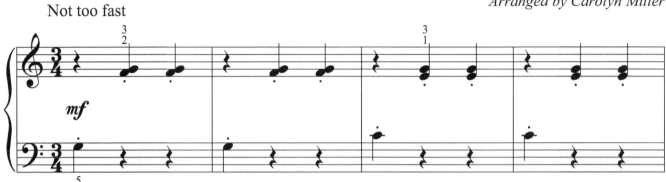

Fine

Arthur de Lulli is a pseudonym for Euphemia Allen, a 16-year-old British girl, who published this famous piece in 1877.

Chopsticks

PRIMO

By Arthur de Lulli
Arranged by Carolyn Miller

Play both hands one octave higher.

Not too fast

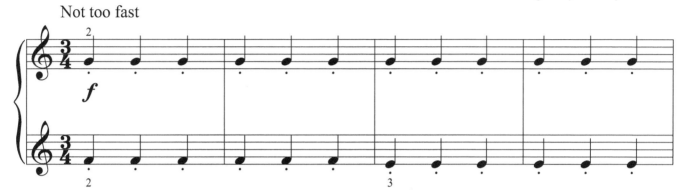

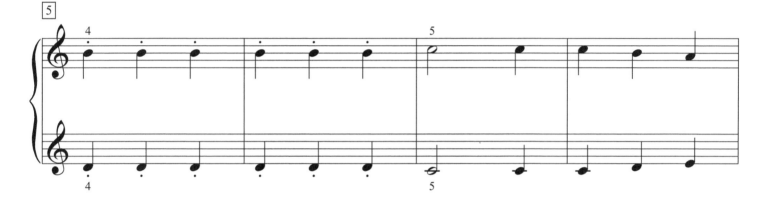

Fine

SECONDO

D.C. al Fine

PRIMO

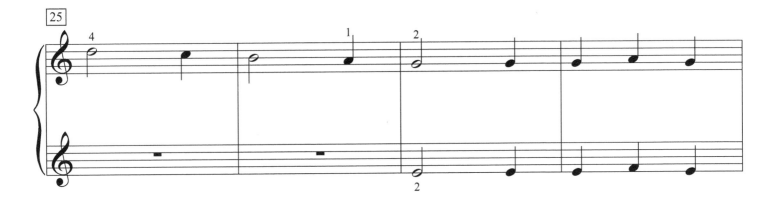

D.C. al Fine

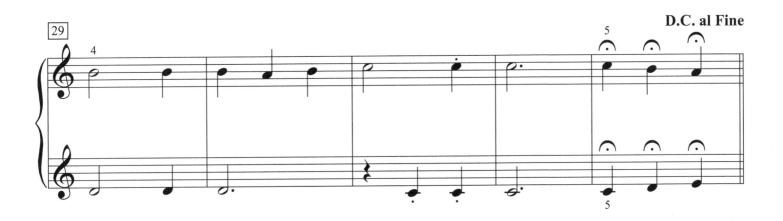

I've Been Working on the Railroad

SECONDO

Play both hands one octave lower.

American Folk Song
Arranged by Carolyn Miller

Moderato, with a bounce!

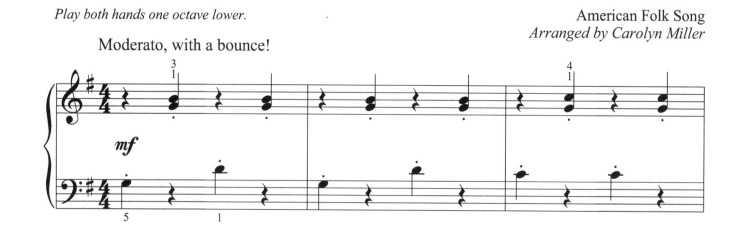

I've Been Working on the Railroad

PRIMO

Play both hands one octave higher.

American Folk Song
Arranged by Carolyn Miller

Moderato, with a bounce!

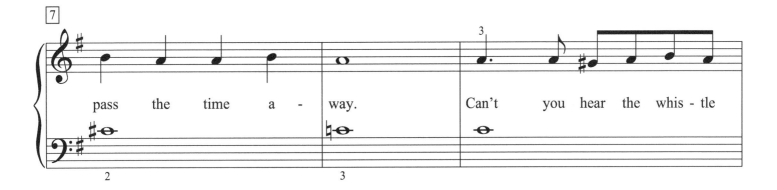

Lyrics: I've been wor-king on the rail-road, all the live-long day. I've been wor-king on the rail-road, just to pass the time a-way. Can't you hear the whis-tle blow-in'? Rise up so ear-ly in the morn.

14

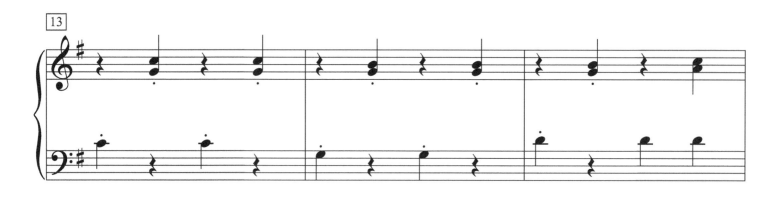

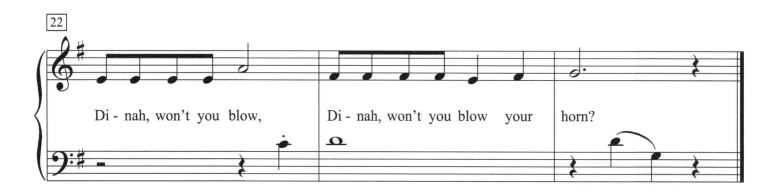

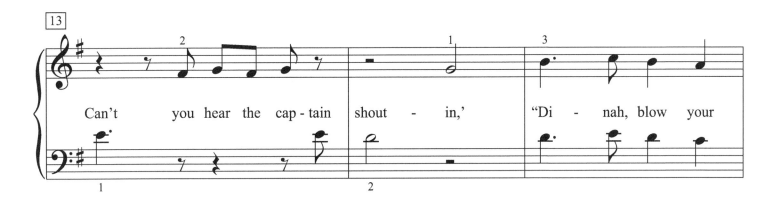

Can't   you hear the cap - tain   shout - in,'   "Di - nah, blow your

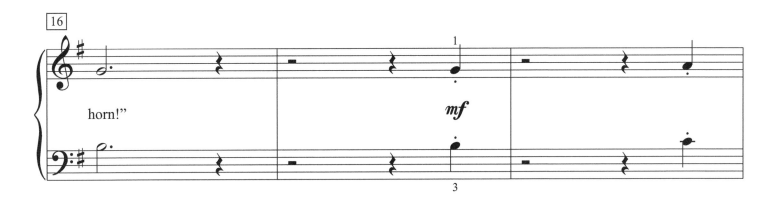

horn!"   mf

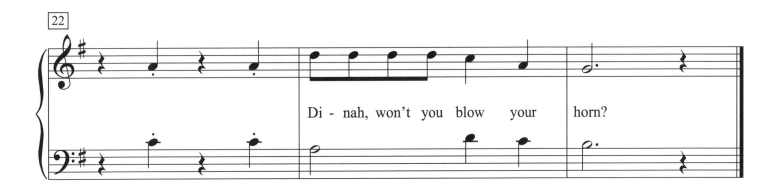

Di - nah, won't you blow   your   horn?

The Yellow Rose of Texas

SECONDO

Play both hands one octave lower.

Words and Music by J.K., 1858
Arranged by Carolyn Miller

With a lilt

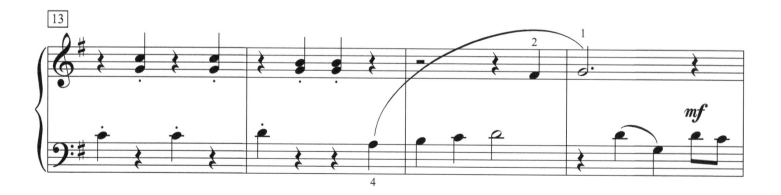

The Yellow Rose of Texas

PRIMO

Play both hands one octave higher.

Words and Music by J.K., 1858
Arranged by Carolyn Miller

With a lilt

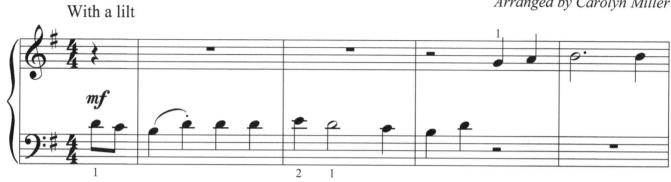

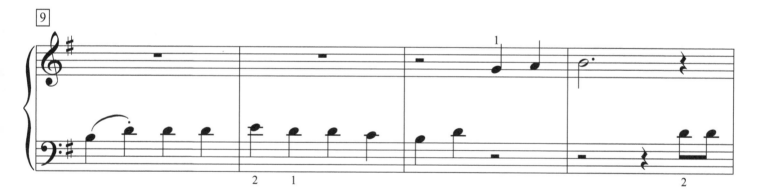

SECONDO

17 *(Keep both hands one octave lower.)*

21

25

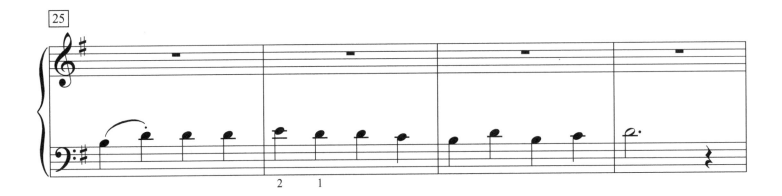

29

mp　　　　　　　　　　　　*poco rit.*

Skip to My Lou

SECONDO

Play both hands one octave lower.

Traditional
Arranged by Carolyn Miller

Happily

Lost my part - ner, what will I do? Lost my part - ner, what will I do?

Lost my part - ner, what will I do? Skip to the Lou, my dar - ling!

Skip to My Lou

PRIMO

Play both hands one octave higher.

Traditional
Arranged by Carolyn Miller

Happily

mf

Choose your part- ners, skip to my Lou. Choose your part- ners, skip to my Lou.

Choose your part- ners, skip to my Lou. Skip to the Lou, my dar - ling!

mp

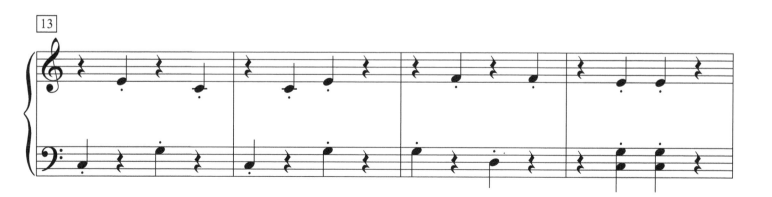

SECONDO

Blow the Man Down

SECONDO

Play both hands one octave lower.

Traditional Sea Chantey
Arranged by Carolyn Miller

With energy

Blow the Man Down

PRIMO

Play both hands one octave higher.

Traditional Sea Chantey
Arranged by Carolyn Miller

With energy

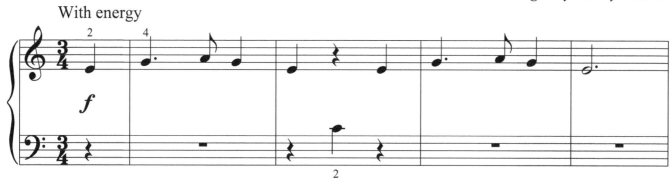

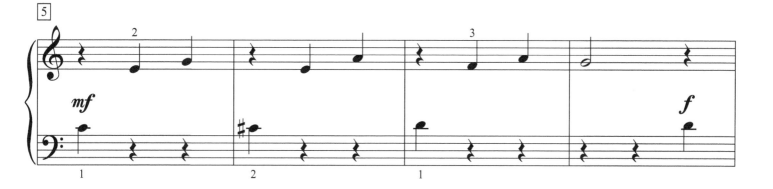

SECONDO

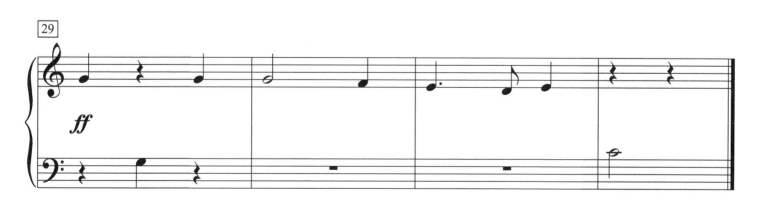

Short'nin' Bread

SECONDO

Play both hands one octave lower.

Plantation Song
Arranged by Carolyn Miller

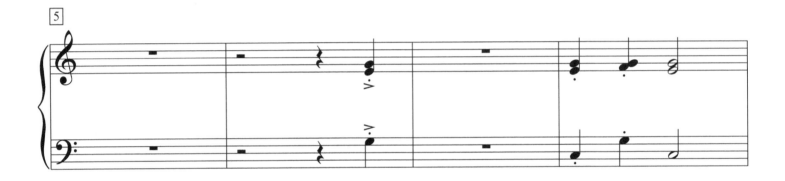

Short'nin' Bread

PRIMO

Play both hands one octave higher.

Plantation Song
Arranged by Carolyn Miller

Put on the skil-let, put on the lead, Mam-my's gon-na bake a lit-tle short-'nin' bread.

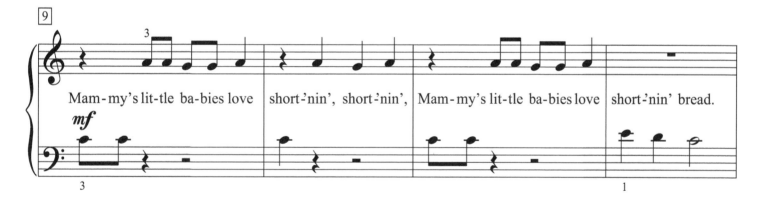

That ain't all she's gon-na do, Mam-my's gon-na make a pot of cof-fee, too.

Mam-my's lit-tle ba-bies love short-'nin', short-'nin', Mam-my's lit-tle ba-bies love short-'nin' bread.

Mam-my's lit-tle ba-bies love short-'nin', short-'nin', Mam-my's lit-tle ba-bies love short-'nin' bread!

A Bicycle Built for Two
(Daisy Bell)

SECONDO

Play both hands one octave lower.

Words and Music by Harry Dacre
Arranged by Carolyn Miller

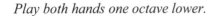

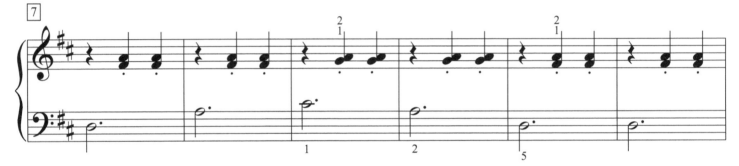

A Bicycle Built for Two
(Daisy Bell)

PRIMO

Play both hands one octave higher.

Words and Music by Harry Dacre
Arranged by Carolyn Miller

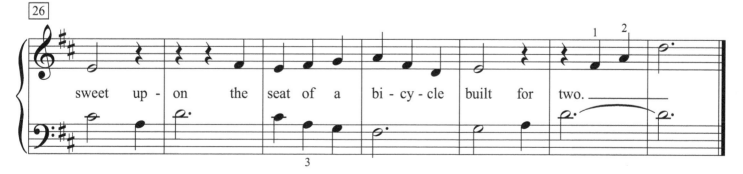

TEACHING LITTLE FINGERS TO PLAY MORE

TEACHING LITTLE FINGERS TO PLAY MORE
by Leigh Kaplan
Teaching Little Fingers to Play More is a fun-filled and colorfully illustrated follow-up book to *Teaching Little Fingers to Play*. It strengthens skills learned while carefully easing the transition into John Thompson's *Modern Course, First Grade*.
00406137 Book only $6.99
00406527 Book/Audio $9.99

SUPPLEMENTARY SERIES
All books include optional teacher accompaniments.

BROADWAY SONGS
arr. Carolyn Miller
MID TO LATER ELEMENTARY LEVEL
10 great show tunes for students to enjoy, including: Edelweiss • I Whistle a Happy Tune • I Won't Grow Up • Maybe • The Music of the Night • and more.
00416928 Book only $6.99
00416929 Book/Audio $12.99

CHILDREN'S SONGS
arr. Carolyn Miller
MID-ELEMENTARY LEVEL
10 songs: The Candy Man • Do-Re-Mi • I'm Popeye the Sailor Man • It's a Small World • Linus and Lucy • The Muppet Show Theme • Sesame Street Theme • Supercalifragilisticexpialidocious • Tomorrow.
00416810 Book only $6.99
00416811 Book/Audio $12.99

CLASSICS
arr. Randall Hartsell
MID-ELEMENTARY LEVEL
7 solos: Marche Slave • Over the Waves • Polovtsian Dance (from the opera *Prince Igor*) • Pomp and Circumstance • Rondeau • Waltz (from the ballet *Sleeping Beauty*) • William Tell Overture.
00406760 Book only $5.99
00416513 Book/Audio $10.99

DISNEY TUNES
arr. Glenda Austin
MID-ELEMENTARY LEVEL
9 songs, including: Circle of Life • Colors of the Wind • A Dream Is a Wish Your Heart Makes • A Spoonful of Sugar • Under the Sea • A Whole New World • and more.
00416750 Book only $9.99
00416751 Book/Audio $12.99

EASY DUETS
arr. Carolyn Miller
MID-ELEMENTARY LEVEL
9 equal-level duets: A Bicycle Built for Two • Blow the Man Down • Chopsticks • Do Your Ears Hang Low? • I've Been Working on the Railroad • The Man on the Flying Trapeze • Short'nin' Bread • Skip to My Lou • The Yellow Rose of Texas.
00416832 Book only $6.99
00416833 Book/Audio $10.99

JAZZ AND ROCK
Eric Baumgartner
MID-ELEMENTARY LEVEL
11 solos, including: Big Bass Boogie • Crescendo Rock • Funky Fingers • Jazz Waltz in G • Rockin' Rhythm • Squirrel Race • and more!
00406765 Book only $5.99

MOVIE MUSIC
arr. Carolyn Miller
LATER ELEMENTARY LEVEL
10 magical movie arrangements: Bella's Lullaby (Twilight) • Somewhere Out There (An American Tail) • True Love's Kiss (Enchanted) • and more.
00139190 Book/Audio $10.99

Also available:

AMERICAN TUNES
arr. Eric Baumgartner
MID-ELEMENTARY LEVEL
00406755 Book only $6.99

BLUES AND BOOGIE
Carolyn Miller
MID-ELEMENTARY LEVEL
00406764 Book only $5.99

CHRISTMAS CAROLS
arr. Carolyn Miller
MID-ELEMENTARY LEVEL
00406763 Book only $6.99

CHRISTMAS CLASSICS
arr. Eric Baumgartner
MID-ELEMENTARY LEVEL
00416827 Book only $6.99
00416826 Book/Audio $12.99

CHRISTMAS FAVORITES
arr. Eric Baumgartner
MID-ELEMENTARY LEVEL
00416723 Book only $7.99
00416724 Book/Audio $12.99

FAMILIAR TUNES
arr. Glenda Austin
MID-ELEMENTARY LEVEL
00406761 Book only $6.99

HYMNS
arr. Glenda Austin
MID-ELEMENTARY LEVEL
00406762 Book only $6.99

JEWISH FAVORITES
arr. Eric Baumgartner
MID-ELEMENTARY LEVEL
00416755 Book only $5.99

RECITAL PIECES
Carolyn Miller
MID-ELEMENTARY LEVEL
00416540 Book only $5.99

SONGS FROM MANY LANDS
arr. Carolyn C. Setliff
MID-ELEMENTARY LEVEL
00416688 Book only $5.99

WILLIS MUSIC

EXCLUSIVELY DISTRIBUTED BY

HAL•LEONARD®

Complete song lists online at
www.halleonard.com